First Person

A ★ M ★ E ★ R ★ I ★ C ★ A

THE
STRUGGLE
TO GROW

Expansionism and Industrialization (1880-1913)

Gene Brown

Twenty-First Century Books

A Division of Henry Holt and Company
New York

Twenty-First Century Books
A Division of Henry Holt and Company, Inc.
115 West 18th Street
New York, New York 10011

Henry Holt® and colophon are registered trademarks of Henry Holt
and Company, Inc.
Publishers since 1866

Published in Canada by Fitzhenry & Whiteside Ltd.
195 Allstate Parkway, Markham, Ontario L3R 4T8

Printed in the United States of America
All first editions are printed on acid-free paper ∞.

Created and produced in association with Blackbirch Graphics, Inc.

Library of Congress Cataloging-in-Publication Data

Brown, Gene.
    The struggle to grow: expansionism and industrialism, 1880–1913/
Gene Brown.— 1st edition.
        p.   cm. — (First person America)
    Includes bibliographical references and index.
    Summary: Primary source materials present life on the Western
frontier, urbanization, immigration, social reformers, and contemporary
technology.
     ISBN 0-8050-2584-7 (alk. paper)
     1.United States—History—1865–1921—Sources—Juvenile literature.
    [1. United States—History—1865–1921—Sources.] I. Title. II. Series.
E661.B82 1993
973.8—dc20   93-24992
                                                              CIP

CONTENTS

Newly arrived immigrants admire the Statue of Liberty in New York Harbor in the late 1800s (*Library of Congress*).

INTRODUCTION

The Civil War, in which the North fought the South and emerged victorious, ended in 1865. It determined the direction that civil rights and social equality would take in the years to come.

After the war, the South, which had been primarily an agricultural society, was faced with severe economic problems. The war had ruined Southern agriculture— many plantations had been destroyed, the system of slave labor had been abolished, and landowners did not have the money to buy seed and equipment or to pay workers. In addition, the Southern transportation system was in ruins, so it was difficult to get crops to market. Despite all this, Southerners tried to rebuild their economy through agricultural endeavors, but they continued to be troubled by problems.

Meanwhile, the North increased its power as a successful manufacturing center. Many Northerners had money to invest in new businesses; cheap labor was available as a result of immigration; and efficient means of transportation were already available. The North prospered, while the South struggled to survive.

The changes in society that took place in the years following the Civil War raised many questions. Could expansion and change go on indefinitely? What would nonstop growth do to the land and its people? How could Americans cope with the fact that the benefits of this growth were not being shared equally? What might happen if this spirit of expansion led America to move beyond its own boundaries, making its strength felt abroad?

The image that Americans had of their country no longer fit the "new" nation that the United States had become. Our system of government was set up to run a much simpler, smaller country. The society that had given birth to this system had passed. Adjustments would be needed.

What would be the consequences of letting "foreigners" cross America's boundaries in a time of unlimited immigration? Would America remain the same country if various segments of the population could not speak English and had ideas and customs that differed from those of their neighbors?

Could the country hold together if the gap between rich and poor grew wider? Would people continue to have faith in democracy if it was applied unequally— to African Americans and women, for example?

Sculptor Auguste Bartholdi (below, center) supervises the application of plaster to the Statue of Liberty's wooden left-hand support. The plaster version was used to cast the copper pieces for the final statue (*Library of Congress*).

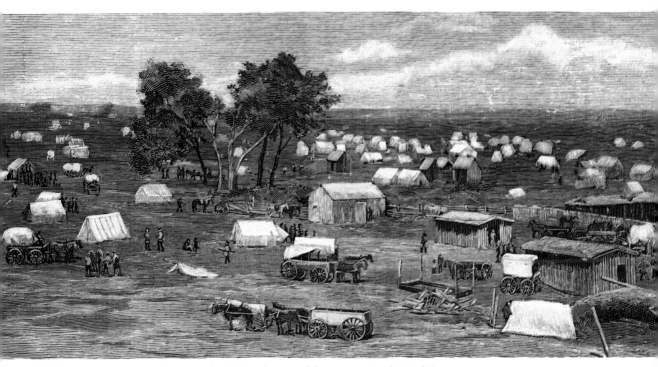

Oklahoma City, soon after it was founded at the turn of the century (*North Wind Picture Archives*).

To much of the world, America meant abundance—an unlimited supply of almost everything, beginning with the land itself. The promise of a life of plenty drew people to these shores from all over. It motivated them to make the long and sometimes dangerous journey to begin a new life.

The West, with its wide open spaces, was a symbol of this natural wealth. By the late nineteenth century, however, the wide open spaces were being filled. Warnings were being sounded that there was, after all, a limit to how much the earth could give up. In these warnings we see the emergence of the movement to preserve the environment.

A popular idea at the beginning of the twentieth century was that America would be a "melting pot."

This view held that people from all nations could blend in, enriching our society with their contributions as they lost the characteristics that made them different and became Americans.

Most often this did happen, but not without many problems and a great deal of pain. New immigrants experienced prejudice from people who had already been here a while. Immigrant groups clashed with one another. Gradually, the idea would arise that everyone did not have to be "as American as apple pie." There could be room as well for Jewish knishes, Italian cannoli, Polish kielbasa, and Irish soda bread.

Millions came to America in the late 1800s and the first part of the twentieth century with the idea that they could make a decent living and that their children would do even better. This was true for enough people to keep the immigrants flowing into the nation's ports. The majority, however, would find opportunities more limited than they had expected. Working conditions could be terrible. And the "captains of industry," who ran American factories, would sometimes have as much power over immigrants as the aristocracies in the lands they had left. What was to be done about this?

For Thomas Jefferson (1743–1826), the American farm had been the ideal basis for democracy. But by the 1890s, farmers were being crushed between falling prices for their crops and rising prices for the manufactured goods they bought. For them, the American dream was turning into a nightmare. Their response was a movement called populism.

What about political and social inequality? While the Civil War had settled the issue of slavery, it did not solve the problem of how to get white America to treat former slaves and other people of color as equals. What

BUFFALO BILL'S WILD WEST

AND CONGRESS OF ROUGH RIDERS OF THE WORLD.

COL. W. F. CODY
BUFFALO BILL
WILL APPEAR
AT EVERY PERFORMANCE

CONGRESS OF AMERICAN INDIANS, REPRESENTING VARIOUS TRIBES, CHARACTERS AND PECULIARITIES OF THE WILY DUSKY WARRIORS IN SCENES F ACTUAL LIFE GIVING THEIR WEIRD WAR DANCES AND PICTURESQUE STYLE OF HORSEMANSH

was the solution to this conflict between American ideals and the reality of a very imperfect society?

The selections included in this book deal with the many problems that would underlie American society during the twentieth century: national expansion versus conservation, urban versus rural interests, labor versus capital, and limited government versus a need to protect minorities and people in general from oppression. These selections will give you a feeling of what it was like for Americans to grapple with these problems as part of their lives.

A poster advertises Buffalo Bill's Wild West Show, one of the most popular entertainments of the late nineteenth century (*Library of Congress*).

A Texas cattle herder stops for a rest on the open plains of America's Southwest (*North Wind Picture Archives*).

CHAPTER 1

THE FRONTIER DEVELOPS

The Cowboy: A Difficult Life

Real cowboys of the Old West would have been surprised to see how they have been portrayed in novels and movies. It is true that the land on which they worked was often beautiful—they did ride in the "wide open spaces"—but their work was also hard, dirty, and dangerous. As cowboy Andy Adams relates in the following selection from his log about a cattle drive that began on April 1, 1882, there was nothing romantic about the work of a cowboy. It was a business in which much could, and did, go wrong. Large sums of money were tied up in the cattle—if they didn't get to their destination safely, the herd's owner could go broke, and many jobs would be lost.

The beautiful scenery was often one of the cowboy's greatest enemies. Rivers, for example, could be difficult obstacles, threatening the lives of people and animals. In fact, water played a big part in cattle drives, as it did in so much else in the West. This was,

Tough men were needed to keep the peace on the frontier. Pictured here are some of Dodge City's most respected lawmen, including Wyatt Earp (front row, second from left) and Bat Masterson (back row, right). This is the only known photograph of these famous lawmen together (*National Archives*).

of course, before pipelines and irrigation ditches criss-crossed this section of the country. The scarcity of water, as described in the account, affected almost everything the cowboys did.

This cattle drive came near the end of an era. With railroads stretching gradually into every corner of the West and ranches established throughout the area, it became less necessary to herd cattle over great distances. Blizzards in January 1886 threatened many cattlemen with bankruptcy. Prices for cattle later dropped, making it uneconomical to risk the losses of the trail drive for such a small profit. Gradually, a way of life was lost, and the legends began.

From the Log of Cowboy Andy Adams

The outlook was anything but encouraging. Flood and Forrest scouted the creek up and down for ten miles in a fruitless search for water. The outfit held the herd back until the twilight of evening, when Flood returned and confirmed McCann's report. It was twenty miles yet to the next water ahead, and if the horse stock could only be watered thoroughly, Flood was determined to make the attempt to nurse the herd through to water. McCann was digging an extra well, and he expressed the belief that by hollowing out a number of holes, enough water could be secured for the saddle stock. Honeyman had corralled the horses and was letting only a few go to the water at a time, while the night horses were being thoroughly watered as fast as the water rose in the well.

Holding the herd this third night required all hands. Only a few men at a time were allowed to go into camp and eat, for the herd refused even to lie down. What few cattle attempted to rest were prevented by the more restless ones. By spells they would mill, until riders were sent through the herd at a break-neck pace to break up the groups. During these milling efforts of the herd, we drifted over a mile from camp; but by the light of moon and stars and the number of riders, scattering was prevented. As the horses were loose for the night, we could not start them on the trail until daybreak gave us a change of mounts, so we lost the early start of the morning before.

Good cloudy weather would have saved us, but in its stead was a sultry morning without a breath of air, which bespoke another day of sizzling heat.

We had not been on the trail over two hours before the heat became almost unbearable to man and beast. Had it not been for the condition of the herd, all might yet have gone well; but over three days had now elapsed without water for the cattle, and they became feverish and ungovernable.... Our horses were fresh, however, and after about two hours' work, we once more got the herd strung out in trailing fashion; but before a mile had been covered, the leaders again turned, and the cattle congregated into a mass of unmanageable animals, milling and lowing in their fever and thirst.... After wasting several hours in this manner, they finally turned back over the trail, and the utmost efforts of every man in the outfit failed to check them. We threw our ropes in their faces, and when this failed, we resorted to shooting; but in defiance of the fusillade and the smoke they walked sullenly through the line of horsemen across their front. Six-shooters were discharged so close to the leaders' faces as to singe their hair, yet, under a noonday sun, they disregarded this and every other device to turn them, and passed wholly out of our control. In a number of instances wild steers deliberately walked against our horses, and then for the first time a fact dawned on us that chilled the marrow in our bones,—*the herd was going blind.*

The bones of men and animals that lie bleaching along the trails abundantly testify that this was not the first instance in which the plain had baffled the determination of man. It was now evident that nothing short of water would stop the herd, and we rode aside and let them pass.

From: *The Log of a Cowboy* by Andy Adams (Boston and New York: Houghton Mifflin Co., 1903).

Pioneering Women

A pioneer family pauses
in Loup Valley, Nebraska,
in 1886 (*National
Archives*).

T he previous selection portrays
the Old West through the eyes of a man, as is generally
the case in television and movies as well. It's the
cowboy riding herd, the rancher galloping across his
land, the lawman chasing outlaws, and the saloon-
keeper trying to keep order in his place on a Saturday
night. But families, not isolated individuals, settled

the West. The wagon trains that brought them were filled with women and children.

As can be seen in the following selection by Mrs. C. A. Teeples, most women who went West and wrote about it focused on their homes and the threat that disease posed to their children. This often made up a woman's world at the time.

Mrs. Teeples belonged to the Mormon religious sect. The Mormons moved West as the result of the teachings of their religious leaders, who believed it was their mission to find a new promised land.

No matter what things were like back East, western women had to get used to living a rougher life in their new home. Logs and mud were basic construction materials, as Mrs. Teeples describes in her account of pioneer life in Arizona. A two-room house was a luxury for pioneers in this period.

While crime in the streets was not a problem, because there were no streets in most places, there was little law and order, so a woman could not walk safely alone in many areas. This was a good reason for women to become experts with a rifle, as so many did.

Mrs. Teeples writes almost matter-of-factly about losing her son to malaria. This doesn't mean that she didn't love him as much as a modern woman would love her child. It's simply a testimony to the fact that death was ever present in the pioneers' West. Getting to a doctor often took a day or more. Even when doctors were nearby, there were few things they could do to treat diphtheria and the many other diseases that adults and children contracted. In addition, frequent accidents occurred. Saws, hammers, and other tools were in constant use because almost everything had to be built from scratch.

Inside a typical covered wagon, 1849 (*National Archives*).

The World of Mrs. Teeples

Tents were pitched and a townsite laid out into lots, and the men drew tickets for their lots, which were numbered. Each man went on his lot and went to work to improve it. They went to the river and cut cottonwood logs with which to build their houses, and exchanged work in building them. Mr. Teeples' house was the first one built with windows, doors and floors. This one was built with two rooms, with a shed between.

Mr. Teeples had a good blacksmith shop and the ranchers often came to have their tools repaired; travelers would also stop for meals. Some were clothed like human beings, but had the manners of beasts—as wicked as sin could make them, and those who were with them who would be decent, were afraid to object to their actions for fear of death. One time a gang got into a fight, beat one man until they thought him dead, then rode off and left him. Later, some of them came back and found him still alive and asked our people to care for him.... Other things were very trying. Our cattle at one time all went blind and our men had a hard time to cure them from this infection. At times the Indians were so bad that some of the men would have to stand guard at night.

Many families came the first fall and winter. Some only remained a short time and then went to St. David, where they could get freighting as employment. Our men bought a threshing machine and threshed their own grain and hauled it, thus keeping them in employment. They made their own flour at a great saving, as at that time flour was eight dollars a hundred. We would get four pounds of sugar for one dollar and other groceries were priced on the same basis. While the men were threshing they contracted malarial fever and were very sick. Mr. Wilton Hawes, whose wife had died before he left Utah, was living on Mrs. Patterson's ranch. He had a large family and they all took the fever and chills, and his daughter narrowly escaped death. Mrs. S. G. Rogers and I were called to go and care for this girl. We stayed all day, and worked with her until she was out of danger.... The next morning (Saturday) my son took sick with the same malady, and on Sunday he died. At this time we were threatened with having our stock driven off and ourselves driven out on foot. But we weathered it in spite of all the discouragements and trials.

From: *Let Them Speak for Themselves: Women in the American West 1849–1900*, Christiane Fischer, ed. (Hamden, Connecticut: Shoe String Press, 1977). Copyright © Christiane Fischer. Reprinted by permission.

Conserving the Nation's Resources

The explorers who first saw the New World were struck by the abundance of natural resources and wildlife. Whatever people might need was there for the taking. So thick and rich was the forest, for example, that it was said that a monkey might swing for hundreds of miles across the treetops before having to come down.

For the first few centuries of our national life, Americans acted as if there really were no end to the land, trees, minerals, and other resources that we now know to be endangered. By the late nineteenth century, however, with a steadily increasing population and the end of the frontier, the idea of limits began to spread. Some people started to wonder what kind of America might be handed on to future generations if care was not taken with our natural wealth.

In 1887, the Division of Forestry was established in the Department of Agriculture. Within a few years, Congress gave the president the power to set aside forest preserves on government land. Funds began to flow from Washington to the states for conservation.

The first public figure to become associated with the conservation movement was Theodore Roosevelt (1858–1919). He spent part of his adult life in the West, operating a cattle ranch in the Dakota territory. There he developed a love and respect for the outdoors that he brought to his presidency in 1901.

Teddy Roosevelt made it clear to the American people that conservation was a major issue. By the

Theodore Roosevelt
(*U.S. Bureau of Printing and Engraving*).

time he left office, he had added 150 million acres to the national forests. Perhaps more important, Roosevelt took the lead in educating Americans about their environment. The following passage from one of his speeches to Congress demonstrates his concern over the country's natural resources.

Roosevelt followed up this speech with a White House Conservation Conference, which resulted in the formation of a National Conservation Commission. The work he set in motion continues today with concerned citizens and government at local, state, and national levels developing guidelines and implementing programs to protect the environment.

Theodore Roosevelt on Conservation

As a nation we not only enjoy a wonderful measure of present prosperity but if this prosperity is used aright it is an earnest of future success such as no other nation will have. The reward of foresight for this nation is great and easily foretold. But there must be the look ahead, there must be a realization of the fact that to waste, to destroy, our natural resources, to skin and exhaust the land instead of using it so as to increase its usefulness, will result in undermining in the days of our children the very prosperity which we ought by right to hand down to them amplified and developed. For the last few years, through several agencies, the government has been endeavoring to get our people to look ahead and to substitute a planned and orderly development of our resources in place of a haphazard striving for immediate profit.

Optimism is a good characteristic, but if carried to an excess it becomes foolishness. We are prone to speak of the resources of this country as inexhaustible; this is not so. The mineral wealth of the country, the coal, iron, oil, gas, and the like, does not reproduce itself, and therefore is certain to be exhausted ultimately; and wastefulness in dealing with it today means that our descendants will feel the exhaustion a generation or two before they otherwise would.

From: Roosevelt's speech to Congress, 1907. Public record.

This photograph, by famous photographer Lewis Hine, shows a family of Italian immigrants as they arrived on New York's Ellis Island in 1905 (*AP/Wide World Photos*).

CHAPTER 2

A NATION
OF IMMIGRANTS

From Ellis Island:
A Cry for Help

Ellis Island, now a national monument in New York Harbor, is where millions of Europeans first set foot on American soil. After the conditions they had known back home, many regarded the island as the gateway to paradise. But for others, as the following letter tells, conditions were difficult, and the future seemed uncertain.

The letter, written in July of 1909, comes from *The Forward*, a newspaper published on New York City's Lower East Side. The paper was written in Yiddish for its Jewish readers, many of whom were immigrants themselves and thus could sympathize with the difficulties of the man who wrote the letter.

The workers at the immigrant-processing center on Ellis Island seemed to reflect the attitudes that

23

New York's East Side, around 1910 (*Library of Congress*).

many Americans had toward newcomers. They were wary of the immigrants' "foreign" ways and suspected that they might be harboring Old World diseases and perhaps Old World political ideas that would not fit in here. Those working on the island didn't even like foreign names and would change them whenever they could. *Smokowski* might become *Smith*, for example.

A major effort was made to keep out people whose politics were judged too "radical" for America, as well as those who might not be able to support themselves—or be supported by a friend or relative already living in the United States.

Even more efforts were devoted to limiting entry to those who were healthy. If an inspector thought an immigrant had a disease, he would place a dreaded chalk mark on the person's coat. This alerted other inspectors down the line to put this person in quarantine (isolation), or worse, to put the sick immigrant on the first ship going back to Europe. It happened often, sometimes even splitting up families.

For most immigrants, Ellis Island *was* a doorway to opportunity. But there was sometimes a high price to pay for entry, as this letter makes clear.

Letter of a Disillusioned Immigrant

Dear Editor,

We, the unfortunates who are imprisoned on Ellis Island, beg you to have pity on us and print our letter in your worthy newspaper, so that our brothers in America may know how we suffer here.

The people here are from various countries, most of them are Russian Jews, many of whom can never return to Russia. These Jews are deserters from the Russian army and political escapees, whom the Czar would like to have returned to Russia. Many of the families sold everything they owned to scrape together enough for passage to America.

They haven't a cent but they figured that, with the help of their children, sisters, brothers and friends, they could find means of livelihood in America.

You know full well how much the Jewish immigrant suffers till he gets to America. First he has a hard enough time at the borders, then with the agents. After this he goes through a lot till they send him, like baggage, on the train to a port. There he lies around in the immigrant sheds till the ship finally leaves. Then follows the torment on the ship, where every sailor considers a steerage [cheapest part of the ship] passenger a dog. And when, with God's help, he has endured all this, and he is at least in America, he is given for "dessert" an order that he must show that he possesses twenty-five dollars.

But where can we get it? Who ever heard of such an outrage, treating people so? If we had known before, we would have provided for it somehow back at home. What nonsense this is! We must have the money on arrival, yet a few hours later (when relatives come) it's too late. For this kind of nonsense they ruin so many people and send them back to the place they escaped from.

It is impossible to describe all that is taking place here, but we want to convey at least a little of it. We are packed into a room where there is space for two hundred people, but they have crammed in about a thousand. They don't let us into the yard for a little fresh air. We lie about on the floor in the spittle and filth. We're wearing the same shirts for three or four weeks, because we don't have our baggage with us.

Everyone goes around dejected and cries and wails. Women with little babies, who have come to their husbands, are being detained. Who can stand this suffering? Men are separated from their wives and children and only when they take us out to eat can they see them. When a man wants to ask his wife something, or when a father wants to see his child, they don't let him. Children get sick, they are taken to a hospital, and it often happens that they never come back.

Because today is a holiday, the Fourth of July, they didn't send anyone back. But Tuesday, the fifth, they began again to lead us to the "slaughter," that is, to the boat. And God knows how many Jewish lives this will cost, because more than one mind dwells on the thought of jumping into the water when they take him to the boat.

All our hope is that you, Mr. Editor, will not refuse us, and print our letter which is signed by many immigrants. The women have not signed, because they don't let us get to them.

This letter is written by one of the immigrants, a student from Petersburg University...

Alexander Rudnev
July 4, 1909.

From: *A Bintel Brief,* Isaac Metzker, ed., trans. (New York: Ballantine Books, © 1977). Reprinted by permission.

In Praise of America

Unlike the young Jewish man whose letter appeared in *The Forward*, Mary Antin was thrilled beyond words with what she found in America. Antin came to this country from Russia in 1894, when she was 13 years old. In 1912 she wrote *The Promised Land*, a selection from which follows. In her book, Antin hoped to let native-born Americans see their land through the eyes of an outsider, who appreciated the country more because she knew what life was like elsewhere.

In writing her book, Antin was taking her place in what has become an important tradition in our history. Immigrants have ranked among those individuals who, in their praise of America, have expressed their whole-hearted support for our country and the ideals it stands for. What people born in this country take for granted, those who come from other lands see as a precious gift. That can be something as everyday and familiar as the local library. Free lending libraries opened a world of possibilities for the children of immigrants early in this century. Had they remained in Europe or wherever else they came from, they might have seen only a few books in their entire lives. Because libraries seemed so precious, many immigrant parents made sure their children made good use of them. They also pushed their offspring to do well in the free schools. As a result, by the end of the first decade of the twentieth century, the illiteracy rate among the children of immigrants was lower than that of native-born children.

European immigrants crowd together aboard the SS *Westernland* as it heads toward America. Traveling conditions for most immigrants were harsh and uncomfortable for weeks on end (*The Bettman Archive*).

Coming from lands where it was often hard to make even the barest of livings, the people who crossed oceans to reach this country at the turn of the century were also especially proud of their achievements in starting businesses in America. Achievements in the arts and the professions were also noted and became part of the heritage that immigrants passed on, and of which their descendants remain proud.

Mary Antin: Grateful Immigrant

Anybody who knows Boston knows that the West and North Ends are the wrong ends of that city. They form the tenement district, or, in the newer phrase, the slums of Boston. Anybody who is acquainted with the slums of any American metropolis knows that that is the quarter where poor immigrants foregather, to live, for the most part, as unkempt, half-washed, toiling, unaspiring foreigners; pitiful in the eyes of social missionaries, the despair of boards of health, the hope of ward politicians, the touchstone of American democracy. The well-versed metropolitan knows the slums as a sort of house of detention for poor aliens, where they live on probation till they can show a certificate of good citizenship.

He may know all this and yet not guess how Wall Street, in the West End, appears in the eyes of a little immigrant from Polotzk. What would the sophisticated sight-seer say about Union Place, off Wall Street, where my new home waited for me? He would say that it is no place at all, but a short box of an alley. Two rows of three-story tenements are its sides, a stingy strip of sky is its lid, a littered pavement is the floor, and a narrow mouth its exit.

But I saw a very different picture on my introduction to Union Place. I saw two imposing rows of brick buildings, loftier than any dwelling I had ever lived in. Brick was even on the ground for me to tread on, instead of common earth or boards. Many friendly windows stood open, filled with uncovered heads of women and children. I thought the people were interested in us, which was very neighborly. I looked up to the topmost row of windows, and my eyes were filled with the May blue of an American sky!

Education was free. That subject my father had written about repeatedly, as comprising his chief hope for us children, the essence of American opportunity, the treasure that no thief could touch; not even misfortune or poverty. It was the one thing that he was able to promise us when he sent for us; surer, safer than bread or shelter. On our second day I was thrilled with the realization of what this freedom of education meant. A little girl from across the alley came and offered to conduct us to school. My father was out, but we five between us had a few words of English by this time. We knew the word school. We understood. This child, who had never seen us till yesterday, who could not pronounce our names, who was not much better dressed than we, was able to offer us the freedom of the schools of Boston! No application made, no questions asked, no examinations, rulings, exclusions; no machinations, no fees. The doors stood open for every one of us. The smallest child could show us the way.

This incident impressed me more than anything I had heard in advance of the freedom of education in America. It was a concrete proof—almost the thing itself. One had to experience it to understand it.

From: *The Promised Land* by Mary Antin (Boston: Houghton Mifflin Co., 1912).

Homesteaders traveled great distances across America's vast plains in order to settle unclaimed land at the turn of the century (*North Wind Picture Archives*).

Life in Rural America

It was only natural that many immigrants would settle in the coastal cities of America. It was there, after all, that they landed when they arrived. Many already had relatives in the cities, ready to take them in and start them on the road to becoming Americans. They would also find that cities offered them many opportunities to make a living.

But there were also those newcomers who, having lived on farms back home, wanted to remain farmers in their new land. And there were others who had heard about the vast tracts of cheap land to the west that were producing golden harvests. They thought that the West might offer the best path to wealth.

Hamlin Garland, a writer who grew up in Wisconsin and Iowa, told the story of life in the small towns and on the farms where many of these immigrants settled. Garland wrote short stories, novels, and a multivolume memoir. An excerpt from *A Son of the Middle Border*, the first volume of his memoirs, follows. As can be seen in the beginning of the selection, the process of fitting into this new society was not necessarily easier in rural America than on the city streets. As is often true today, immigrants of all ages tended to stick to their own kind, at least at first.

While it is often comforting to be with people who understand our customs and speak our language, this sometimes leads to tensions with others who live differently. Here it's the Norwegian-American schoolboys contending for "turf" with the local young people,

whose parents may have arrived a decade or two
earlier. The story is familiar throughout our history—
only the names of the foreign countries from which the
immigrants come change.

Garland also makes another important point here.
While tenement life and factory work in the cities, part

Before the telegraph, mail and news traveled across the frontier by Pony Express. Pony Express riders carried information and communications on horseback (*North Wind Picture Archives*).

of the memories of most immigrant groups, could be rough, so, too, could life on a farm. In other parts of this book, Garland often writes about the glories of growing up close to nature. But he did not forget what it was like to have to harvest nature's bounty when your living depended on it.

Hamlin Garland:
Not "the Merry, Merry Farmer"

The school-house of this district stood out upon the prairie to the west a mile distant, and during May we trudged our way over a pleasant road, each carrying a small tin pail filled with luncheon. Here I came in contact with the Norwegian boys from the colony to the north, and a bitter feud arose (or existed) between the "Yankees," as they called us, and "the Norskies," as we called them. Often when we met on the road, showers of sticks and stones filled the air, and our hearts burned with the heat of savage conflict. War usually broke out at the moment of parting....

Most authors in writing of "the merry merry farmer" leave out experiences like this—they omit the mud and the dust and the grime, they forget the army worm, the flies, the heat, as well as the smells and drudgery of the barns. Milking the cows is spoken of in the traditional fashion as a lovely pastoral recreation, when as a matter of fact it is a tedious job. We hated it....

In summer when the flies were particularly savage we had a way of jamming our heads into the cows' flanks to prevent them from kicking into the pail, and sometimes we tied their tails to their legs so that they could not lash our ears.... To the boy who is teaching them to drink out of a pail they are nasty brutes—quite unlike fawns. They have a way of filling their nostrils with milk and blowing it all over their nurse. They are greedy, noisy, ill-smelling and stupid. They look well when running with their mothers in the pasture, but as soon as they are weaned they lose all their charm—for me.

From: *A Son of the Middle Border* by Hamlin Garland (New York: Macmillan Publishing, ©1917). Reprinted by permission.

CHAPTER 3

TECHNOLOGY, INDUSTRY, AND LABOR

I Labor Versus Capital

n the late nineteenth century, the government protected private property rights at all costs. It was one of America's most important national values. Property had gained its high place in the American system in an earlier time. People came to these shores so they could be their own bosses and not have to worry about some aristocrat or greedy monarch seizing whatever he or she wanted without regard to the law. Because of this, private property was seen as a necessary part of a free way of life. Any threat to property rights was thus a threat to freedom.

One hundred years after the founding of our nation, however, the nature of property had changed.

During the late 1800s, it no longer just meant a person owning a small business or farm with perhaps a few employees. Giant corporations with power and influence were dominating the economy, and workers were at their mercy.

But the law protected corporations as if they were still individuals running a small business. Workers needed protection, too, so they organized into unions. Acting as a group, they would have the collective power to speak to their bosses—power that they did not have as individuals. The law, however, often labeled their activities a conspiracy.

This is the background of the Homestead steel strike of 1892, celebrated in the "Song of a Strike," which follows. On June 29 of that year, workers at the Carnegie Steel Company in Homestead, Pennsylvania, struck after Henry Clay Frick, the company's manager, tried to cut workers' wages. Frick hired 300 security guards from the Pinkerton agency to break the strike.

When the Pinkertons arrived on July 6, a bloody battle broke out. Several workers and detectives were killed, and many more were wounded. The Pinkertons were routed. The strike went on, and finally the governor sent in the militia to do what the Pinkertons couldn't. On November 20, the strike was crushed.

This was not the first time that government had sided with the rights of big business over those of working people. Gradually, however, the tide began to change. Public opinion was starting to accept the idea that something had to be done to create a balance of power between labor and capital. In the first two decades of the twentieth century, laws would be passed by both Presidents Theodore Roosevelt and Woodrow

Wilson (1856–1924) to achieve more of a balance. Then, in President Franklin Roosevelt's (1882–1945) New Deal of the 1930s, labor finally came closer to equality with the management of the nation's large corporations. Today we still argue about just how much power management should have and how much weight should be given to the needs of labor.

The Homestead riot broke out in 1892 at the Carnegie Steel Company in Pennsylvania (*North Wind Picture Archives*).

Song of a Strike

We are asking one another as we pass the time of day.
Why workingmen resort to arms to get their proper pay.
And why our labor unions they must not be recognized,
Whilst the actions of a syndicate must not be criticized.
Now the troubles down at Homestead were brought
    about this way,
When a grasping corporation had the audacity to say:
"You must all renounce your union and forswear your
    liberty
And we will give you a chance to live and die in
    slavery."
Now this sturdy band of workingmen started out at the
    break of day,
Determination in their faces which plainly meant to say:
"No one can come and take our homes for which we
    have toiled so long,
No one can come and take our places—no, here's
    where we belong!"
When a lot of bum detectives come without authority,
Like thieves at night when decent men were sleeping
    peacefully—
Can you wonder why all honest hearts with indignation
    burn,
And why the slimy worm that treads the earth when
    trod upon will turn?
When they locked out men at Homestead so they
    were face to face
With a lot of bum detectives and they knew it was
    their place
To protect their homes and families, and this was
    neatly done,
And the public will reward them for the victories
    they won.

From: *Who Built America?*, Vol. 2, Herbert Gutman, et al., eds. (New York: Pantheon Books, 1992). Reprinted by permission.

An American Success Story

America has often been described as the land of opportunity. At the end of the nineteenth century, not only Americans but also much of the world accepted that in this country, if you worked hard, you could make your fortune. If you didn't become rich, they believed, it was your own fault.

Despite the bloody strike at Andrew Carnegie's Homestead plant, which damaged his reputation as an employer, Carnegie became a symbol of what a person could accomplish in America through hard work. Carnegie was born into a poor family in Scotland on November 25, 1835, and came to America in 1848. The telegraph industry was just getting under way, and young Carnegie got in at the beginning. He became an expert telegraph operator and used this skill to get a job working for one of the top executives on the Pennsylvania Railroad.

Carnegie got more business experience during the Civil War and later used what he learned to establish himself in the growing iron-and-steel industry. By slowly building his holdings, he organized his Carnegie Steel Company into a giant New Jersey corporation in 1899. Then, in 1901, he sold the company to J. P. Morgan and others, who made it into the U.S. Steel Corporation. The sale made Carnegie one of the world's richest men.

Having amassed this enormous wealth, Carnegie then set out to help others, giving a great deal of money

Steel being made at a factory in Pittsburgh, Pennsylvania in 1886 (*New-York Historical Society*).

to libraries and also establishing foundations that promoted culture, teaching, and international peace. He believed that anyone who is exceptional enough to accumulate riches should use it to benefit others, an idea he set forth in *The Gospel of Wealth* (1900).

Andrew Carnegie also spent time promoting the idea that anyone could do well by seizing the opportunities that came along. In 1885, Carnegie explained this before a group of students at a Pittsburgh commercial college. In his speech, part of which follows, he made the point that whether you are a success or a failure depends on what you are made of, not what kind of family you were born into or what kind of help you may have received in life. Start at the bottom and work hard, and you will reach the top, he believed.

Carnegie's critics have pointed out that the playing field has never been as even as he made it out to be. Many people are born to wealth, and business skills are not equally distributed throughout the population. Also, discrimination (against African Americans and women, for example) plays a role in keeping some people back, and many who rise to the top do so dishonestly, as frequent scandals remind us. It has been pointed out that the "self-made man," the man who makes it on his own, has often had the help of government. Steel, for example, depended on the railroads as customers. The railroads, in turn, got huge amounts of land from the government so they could build their roads.

Still, what Carnegie describes here has happened often enough in this country to make it seem possible— to this day—to millions all over the world. It is the American "success story," one which Andrew Carnegie enjoyed until he died in 1919.

Andrew Carnegie (*National Portrait Gallery*).

Andrew Carnegie:
The Road to Business Success—
A Talk to Young Men

It is well that young men should begin at the beginning and occupy the most subordinate positions. Many of the leading business men of Pittsburgh had a serious responsibility thrust upon them at the very threshold of their career. They were introduced to the broom, and spent the first hours of their business lives sweeping out the office. I notice we have janitors and janitresses now in offices, and our young men unfortunately miss that salutary branch of a business education. But if by chance the professional sweeper is absent any morning the boy who has the genius of the future partner in him will not hesitate to try his hand at the broom.

You may grow impatient, or become discouraged when year by year you float on in subordinate positions. There is no doubt that it is becoming harder and harder as business gravitates more and more to immense concerns, for a young man without capital to get a start for himself, and in this city especially where large capital is essential, it is usually difficult. Still, let me tell you for your encouragement, that there is no country in the world, where able and energetic young men can so readily rise as this, nor any city where there is more room at the top. Young men give all kinds of reasons why in their cases failure was clearly attributable to exceptional circumstances which render success impossible. Some never had a chance, according to their own story. This is simply nonsense.

From: "An Address to Curry Commercial College, Pittsburgh, June 23, 1885." Published in *The Empire of Business* by Andrew Carnegie (New York: Doubleday, Page, and Co., 1902).

Child Labor: An Abusive Practice

Andrew Carnegie did not talk about the large number of people who made his success possible—the workers in his steel mills, for example, whose wages were kept low and whose working conditions were dangerous enough to maim and kill many of them. These conditions were not regulated, and there were no disability payments for those injured on the job.

Nor did those who celebrated the self-made man dwell on the army of child labor that toiled silently. Child labor in factories began with England's industrial revolution in the eighteenth century. By the start of the twentieth century in the United States, the use of child labor was coming into question. People were horrified by the terrible conditions under which children worked in America's big cities. There was a growing sense that this practice did not fit the idea of progress and the life of a "modern" society.

The realization that children were more than miniature adults was most probably an important influence for change: people saw that children had special needs that were related to their age. Treating children like adults, they thought, might be damaging.

The movement to investigate and curb child labor was strong in Chicago, Illinois, where Jane Addams (1860–1935), a social reformer, had established Hull House in 1889. One of the first settlement houses, it was dedicated to social reform and improving the life of the community. Much of today's social-work movement stems from the Hull House model.

Jane Addams, founder of Chicago's Hull House (*National Portrait Gallery*).

Children at work in a Georgia mill, around 1915 (*National Archives*).

The following selection is from a report on child labor by people associated with Hull House. Given the conditions it describes, it may be surprising that the ban on child labor was still far in the future. A 1916 federal law to regulate it was declared unconstitutional two years later by the Supreme Court. It would be 1938 before Congress finally passed a child-labor law, which was upheld by the Supreme Court in 1941.

Hazards to Life and Health

It is a lamentable fact, well known to those who have investigated child-labor, that children are found in greatest number where the conditions of labor are most dangerous to life and health. Among the occupations in which children are most employed in Chicago, and which most endanger the health, are: The tobacco trade, nicotine poisoning finding as many victims among factory children as among the boys who are voluntary devotees of the weed, consumers of the deadly cigarette included; frame gilding, in which work a child's fingers are stiffened and throat disease is contracted; buttonholing, machine-stitching, and hand-work in tailor or sweat shops, the machine-work producing spinal curvature, and for girls pelvic disorders also, while the unsanitary condition of the shops makes even hand-sewing dangerous; bakeries, where children slowly roast before the ovens; binderies, paper-box and paint factories, where arsenical paper, rotting paste, and the poison of the paints are injurious; boiler-plate works, cutlery works, and metal stamping works, where the dust produces lung disease; the handling of hot metal, accidents; the hammering of plate, deafness. In addition to diseases incidental to trades, there are the conditions of bad sanitation and long hours, almost universal in the factories where children are employed.

From: *Hull-House Maps and Papers* by Residents of Hull House (Boston: Thomas Y. Crowell & Co., 1895). Reprinted by Arno Press, Inc., 1970. Reprinted by permission of Arno Press.

CHAPTER 4

POLITICS AND REFORM

Populism: The People Speak Up

As the abusive practices grew with the expansion of business, reform movements began to take hold. One such movement was populism. The word *populism* means a rising from below, when the people get disgusted with politics as usual and want to take a direct hand in running the government. Populism can represent something as simple as a desire for plain talk in politics and action, not just more empty words. This was present in much of the support for Ross Perot in the presidential campaign of 1992. It can also stand for something deeper and more radical, as it did in the Populist Movement that swept much of the West, Midwest, and South in the 1890s.

The Populist Movement started with the problems of the farmers, who were producing more than their markets could absorb. As a result, the prices farmers received for their crops fell. Meanwhile, a U.S. tariff—a tax on imported goods that was designed to protect

50

American manufacturers—kept prices high on items needed by the general public and those specifically needed by farmers. The low prices on what they sold and the high prices on what they bought meant trouble for farmers.

Feeling that many elected representatives were controlled by the railroads and other large corporations, farmers started coming together in groups to demand change—revolutionary change. They wanted to return to the democracy that had somehow gotten lost with the rise of big business.

The democratic spirit of the Populist Movement was strong. Farmers reached out to labor, which also felt itself a victim of an economy that had passed out of the control of the common person. In the South, for a few years, white and African-American farmers shared a common cause, unusual for the time. The Populists formed a party and ran their own candidate for president in 1892. Some of what they called for has since been adopted, including the direct election of U.S. senators (formerly chosen by state legislatures).

Eventually, however, the movement failed. An improvement in the economy in the second half of the 1890s took some of the steam out of populism. The Democrats ran William Jennings Bryan (1860–1925) for president in 1896, adopting part of the Populist message and winning some support. In the South, wealthy whites played off poor whites against African Americans, destroying their brief moment of unity.

Mary Elizabeth Lease of Kansas was among populism's most fiery speakers. In the following passage from one of her talks, she attacks the wealthy political leaders of the East, accusing them of "white wage slavery" in the South and West.

William Jennings Bryan (*National Portrait Gallery*).

Mary Elizabeth Lease: A Voice for the People

This is a nation of inconsistencies. The Puritans fleeing from oppression became oppressors. We fought England for our liberty and put chains on four million of blacks. We wiped out slavery and our tariff laws and national banks began a system of white wage slavery worse than the first.

Wall Street owns the country. It is no longer a government of the people, by the people, and for the people, but a government of Wall Street, by Wall Street, and for Wall Street.

The great common people of this country are slaves, and monopoly is the master. The West and South are bound and prostrate before the manufacturing East.

Money rules.... Our laws are the output of a system which clothes rascals in robes and honesty in rags.

The [political] parties lie to us and the political speakers mislead us.... The politicians said we suffered from overproduction. Overproduction, when 10,000 little children, so statistics tell us, starve to death every year in the United States, and over 100,000 shopgirls in New York are forced to sell their virtue for the bread their niggardly wages deny them....

We will stand by our homes and stay by our fireside by force if necessary, and we will not pay our debts to the loan-shark companies until the government pays its debts to us. The people are at bay; let the bloodhounds of money who dogged us thus far beware.

From: *History of Kansas, State and People,* W. E. Connelley, ed. (New York: American History Society, 1928).

Segregation and the Civil Rights Movement

Segregation, the separation of whites and African Americans in schools and other public places, did not automatically begin in the South when the slaves gained their freedom. While there was no great mixing of the races, separation was not as complete as it became in the 1890s, when state and local segregation laws were passed. Segregation was also found, less obvious in form, in much of the rest of the country, where custom rather than laws enforced it.

The segregation laws of the 1890s were at least in part a way that the wealthier Southern whites could keep poorer whites from resenting their "betters." With segregation, poor white people didn't have to think of themselves as being at the bottom of the social ladder. For as poor as they might be, whites could always feel superior to African Americans, who were visibly degraded and made to feel worthless.

African-American opposition to segregation began to take shape with the growth of an African-American middle class at the turn of the century. In towns and cities African-American ministers, teachers, and other professionals came together to discuss what they might do about this and an even more pressing problem: lynching and other kinds of violence that whites used to keep African Americans "in their place."

In 1905, W.E.B. Du Bois (1868–1963), who was an African-American scholar and social activist, founded the Niagara Movement to work for change. Four years later, Du Bois, other African Americans, and a number of progressive whites started the NAACP (National Association for the Advancement of Colored People). It was the beginning of the civil rights movement. Early in this struggle, Dr. R. S. Lovingood, who was president of a Texas college for African Americans, wrote a magazine article describing his experiences in a northern city. Published in 1912, this article, which follows, could, unfortunately, have been written 50 years later. As late as the mid-1960s, African-American passengers traveling through the South sat at the back of interstate buses and were not allowed to use the same restrooms or eat at the same lunch counters as the whites traveling with them.

The civil rights laws that were passed during the presidency of Lyndon Johnson (1908–1973) in the 1960s would finally end the legal separation of blacks and whites in the South (and unofficial segregation in other areas). In addition, they would enforce the right of African Americans to vote without being threatened. Dr. Lovingood may have been pleased, but probably not completely satisfied, with the position of African Americans in our society today.

Dr. R. S. Lovingood on
Discrimination in the World

I was in a Northern city recently. I was a stranger. I was hungry. There was food, food on every hand. I had money, and finally I was compelled to feast on a box of crackers and a piece of cheese. I did not ask to eat with the white people, but I did ask to eat.

I was traveling. I got off at a station almost starved. I begged the keeper of a restaurant to sell me a lunch in a paper and hand it out of the window. He refused, and I was compelled to ride a hundred miles farther before I could get a sandwich.

I was in a white church on official business. It was a cold, blowing day, raining, sleeting, freezing. Warm lunch was served in the basement to my white brothers. I could not sit in the corner of that church and eat a sandwich. I had to go nearly two miles in the howling winds and sleet to get a lunch.

I have seen in the South white and black workingmen elbowing each other, eating their lunches at noon and smoking the pipe of peace. Worldly men give me a welcome in their stores. The Government post office serves me without discrimination. But not so in that church run in the name of Jesus.

I could not help but feel that Jesus, too, like me, an unwelcome visitor, was shivering in the cold, and could not find a place in that inn, and was saying: "I was hungered and ye gave me no meat. I was thirsty and you gave me no drink." For Jesus was not an Anglo-Saxon.

I went to a station to purchase my ticket. I was there thirty minutes before the ticket office was opened. When the ticket office opened I at once appeared at the window. While the agent served the white people at the other side I remained there beating the window until the train pulled out. I was compelled to jump on the train without my ticket and wire back to have my trunk expressed to me. Considering the temper of the people, the separate-coach law may be the wisest plan for the conditions in the South, but the statement of "equal accommodations" is all bosh and twaddle. I pay the same money, but I cannot have a chair car, or lavatory, and rarely a through car. I must crawl out all through the night in all kinds of weather, and catch another "Jim Crow" coach. This is not a request to ride with white people. It is a request for justice, for "equal accommodations" for the same money. I made an attempt to purchase some cheap land in a frontier section. The agent told me that the settlers, most of whom were Northerners, would not tolerate a Negro in that section. So I could not purchase it. I protest.

I rode through a small town in Southern Illinois. When the train stopped I went to the car steps to take a view of the country. This is what greeted me: "Look here, darkey, don't get off at this station." I put my head out of the window at a certain small village in Texas, whose reputation was well known to me. This greeted me: "Take your head back, nigger, or we will knock it off."

From: *A Documentary History of the Negro People in the United States,* Vol. 3, Herbert Aptheker, ed. (Secaucus, NJ: Citadel Press, 1977). Copyright © 1973 by Herbert Aptheker. Published in arrangement with Carol Publishing Group.

Alice Paul (second from right) was one of the leaders of the women's suffrage movement who worked to get the Nineteenth Amendment passed by Congress (*AP/ Wide World Photos*).

Suffragism: The Vote for Women

As the twentieth century began, many African Americans, especially in the South, could not vote because local laws made it hard for them to exercise their constitutional rights. In most states, however, women did not have the right to vote at all. The Constitution was no help—it didn't mention them.

When the Constitution was adopted, it specified that qualifications for voting were up to the states. In 1789, the states recognized only one class of voters: free white men who owned property. This finally changed during the 1820s and 1830s, when most states either reduced or abandoned such restrictions. African Americans gained the right to vote in 1870, when the Fifteenth Amendment forbade states from making race a qualification for voting.

By the middle of the nineteenth century, a woman's movement had started. One of its chief demands was that women be allowed to vote. How should they achieve this goal? Some women—and also some men—thought that working to influence each state to change its laws to permit women to vote was the best way. Other suffragists, such as famous activist Alice Paul (1885–1977), said that the best way to get the vote for women was through a constitutional amendment. This, after all, was how African Americans had gained the vote. In 1890, the two groups came together in the National American Woman Suffrage Association. The same year, Wyoming became a state and was the first one to give women the right to vote.

Carrie Chapman Catt (1859–1947), a supporter of women's rights and the president of the National American Woman Suffrage Association, wrote an article that appeared in *The New York Times* on September 3, 1916, part of which follows. That year, Catt's activities and those of other suffragists did not succeed in defeating President Wilson, whose party in Congress had blocked the amendment to give women the right to vote. However, in 1920, their work finally paid off. Wilson was still president when the Nineteenth Amendment granted them their long-sought-after right.

Carrie Chapman Catt: Champion of Women

Because a real crisis has been reached in the woman suffrage movement and because that fact is appreciated by virtually every suffragist in the country, the emergency-called convention of the National American Woman Suffrage Association at Atlantic City next week will be the most important suffrage event which has taken place for many years.

For years we have been saying that suffrage is coming. We said it because we knew. Today we can say that it is here and that it remains only for our women to make one last determined assault upon the opposition to make our victory definite.

Three courses of procedure lie before us. We can concentrate on the Federal amendment; we can drop the Federal amendment and confine our activities to State legislation, or we can continue the present policy of the National American Woman Suffrage Association and work for both State and Federal action.

...The sentiment for nation-wide suffrage grows stronger daily. With this growth in sentiment has come an increased demand for the passage of the Federal suffrage amendment, and because women throughout the country are turning to that Federal amendment for relief from their political disabilities it enters into the political campaign this year with an importance it never had before.

The women of six States will vote for President this year for the first time, and those of six others have the Presidential vote. One group of suffragists has made bold claims that it will persuade enough women within these States to vote against the President, because his party in Congress has blocked the Federal amendment, to defeat him. The audacity and novelty of these claims have piqued the curiosity of some and aroused the angry indignation of others. The main body of suffragists have yet to speak.

It was the National Woman Suffrage Association which introduced the Federal amendment, now discussed as though it were a new discovery, and this was done in 1875. It has been introduced in each succeeding Congress, and ardently supported.

What the Atlantic City convention will determine...remains to be seen. One thing is certain: The confusion, the criss-cross of diverse views on policies and tactics, will be relieved.

The emergency convention will pass into suffrage history as the starting point of the last lap in the long march to victory.

From: *The New York Times*, September 3, 1916, by Carrie Chapman Catt (New York). Copyright ©1916 by The New York Times Company. Reprinted by permission.

Soon after the turn of the century—as the social reforms of Jane Addams, suffragists Alice Paul and Carrie Chapman Catt, and W.E.B. Du Bois began to take hold—America became embroiled in a devastating conflict across the Atlantic. On April 6, 1917, the United States declared war on Germany, thus entering World War I. By the time the war was over, about 10 million soldiers were dead, and about 20 million were wounded. For a while during this period, the social reforms of the recent past were put on hold as America mourned for its dead and looked toward the future for new hope.

FROM VOTING RIGHTS TO WORLD WAR I: 1870–1920

1870
Congress passes the Fifteenth Amendment to the Constitution. For the first time, African Americans in the United States have the right to vote.

1889
Social activist Jane Addams establishes Hull House, one of the first centers in the country dedicated solely to welfare programs and social reform.

1892
A union strike at the Carnegie Steel Company in Homestead, Pennsylvania, turns bloody. Several people are killed and many are injured.

1896
Populist William Jennings Bryan runs for president on the Democratic ticket but loses to William McKinley.

1901
Andrew Carnegie sells Carnegie Steel to J.P. Morgan and others who create U.S. Steel. Carnegie becomes one of the richest men in the world.

1905
W.E.B. DuBois begins the Niagara Movement, one of the earliest nationally organized civil-rights groups. The NAACP emerges four years later.

1908
Theodore Roosevelt, the first major figure in the modern conservation movement, establishes the National Conservation Commission.

1917
The United States officially enters World War I, declaring war on Germany.

1920
The Nineteenth Amendment to the U.S. Constitution is passed, giving women the right to vote.

FOR FURTHER READING

Allen, Robert. *William Jennings Bryan*. Milford, MI: Mott Media, 1992.

Cryan-Hicks, Kathryn. *W.E.B. Du Bois: Crusader for Peace*. Lowell, MA: Discovery Enterprises, 1991.

DeStefano, Susan. *Theodore Roosevelt: Conservation President*. New York: Twenty-First Century Books, 1992.

Fisher, Leonard E. *Ellis Island: Gateway to the New World*. New York: Holiday, 1986.

Freedman, Russell. *Cowboys of the Wild West*. Boston: Clarion Books, 1990.

Markham, Lois. *Theodore Roosevelt*. North Bellmore, NY: Marshall Cavendish, 1991.

Mitchard, Jacquelyn. *Jane Addams: Pioneer in Social Reform and Activist for World Peace*. Milwaukee, WI: Gareth Stevens, 1991.

Reef, Catherine. *Ellis Island*. New York: Dillon, 1991.

Smith, Betsy C. *Women Win the Vote*. Morristown, NJ: Silver Burdett Press, 1989.

Stafford, Mark. *W.E.B. Dubois*. New York: Chelsea House, 1989.

Wheeler, Leslie A. *Jane Addams*. Morristown, NJ: Silver Burdett Press, 1990.

Index